# *My first* EASTER

## Baby Name

Helena Magdelena

Lots of love,
from Nanny & Grandad
xxx

# Warm weather has arrived

# Everything's green again

# The flowers have bloomed

We're very happy.

# The bunny dear and good

Is on his way again

# Many coloured eggs

He brings us all as a gift.

# And let's never forget

# From small to big

That today we celebrate

# The resurrection of the Lord

Today is the feast

Beloved by all

Let us all rejoice

Easter is here again.

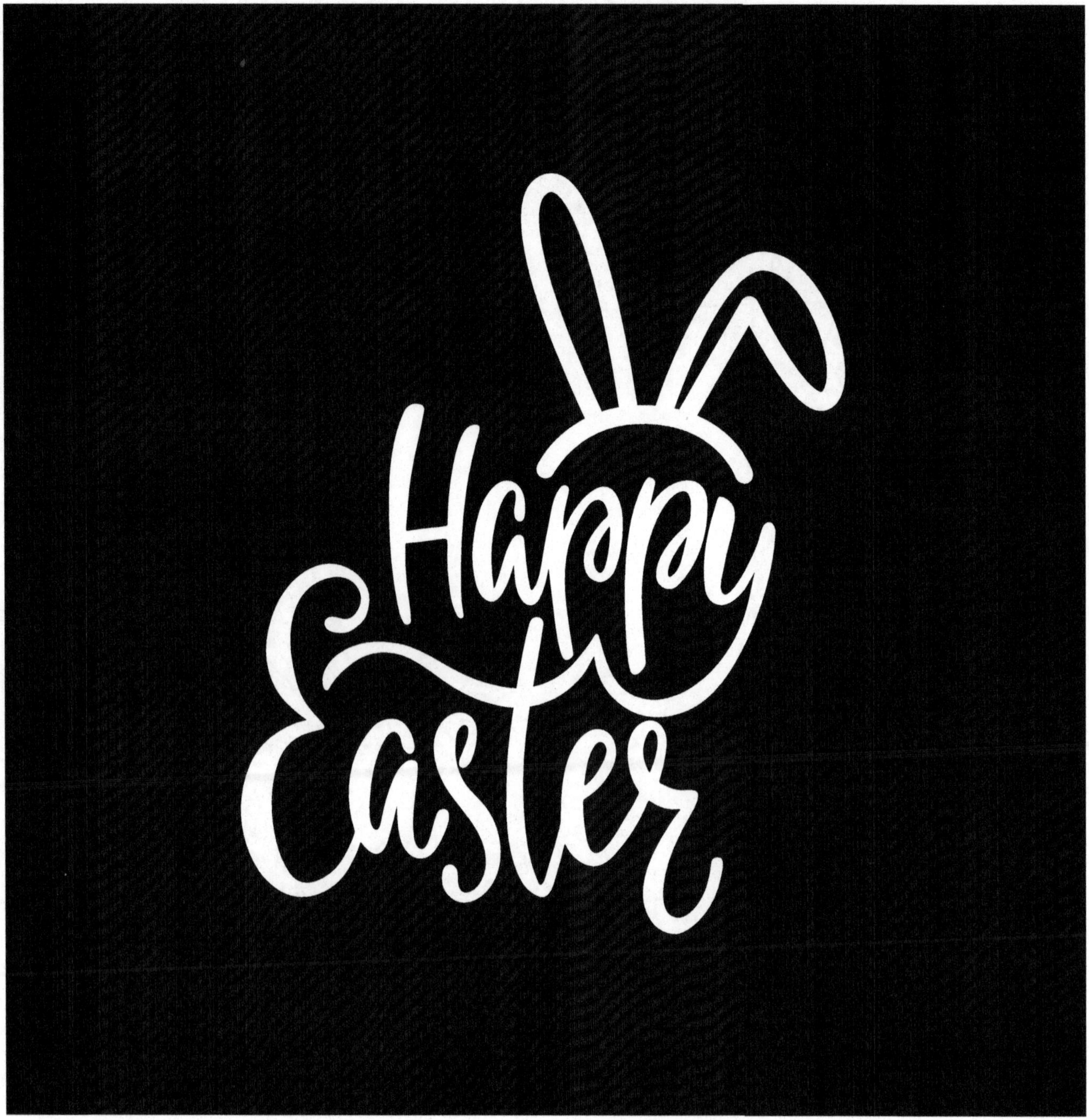
Happy Easter

Printed in Great Britain
by Amazon

20802299R00020